I Spy Books for All Ages:
I SPY: A BOOK OF PICTURE RIDDLES
I SPY CHRISTMAS
I SPY EXTREME CHALLENGER!
I SPY FANTASY
I SPY FUN HOUSE
I SPY GOLD CHALLENGER!
I SPY MYSTERY
I SPY SCHOOL DAYS
I SPY SPOOKY NIGHT
I SPY SUPER CHALLENGER!
I SPY TREASURE HUNT
I SPY ULTIMATE CHALLENGER!
I SPY YEAR-ROUND CHALLENGER!

Books for New Readers:
SCHOLASTIC READER LVL 1: I SPY A BALLOON
SCHOLASTIC READER LVL 1: I SPY A BUTTERFLY
SCHOLASTIC READER LVL 1: I SPY A CANDY CANE
SCHOLASTIC READER LVL 1: I SPY A DINOSAUR'S EYE
SCHOLASTIC READER LVL 1: I SPY A PENGUIN
SCHOLASTIC READER LVL 1: I SPY A PUMPKIN
SCHOLASTIC READER LVL 1: I SPY A SCARY MONSTER
SCHOLASTIC READER LVL 1: I SPY A SCHOOL BUS
SCHOLASTIC READER LVL 1: I SPY FUNNY TEETH
SCHOLASTIC READER LVL 1: I SPY LIGHTNING IN THE SKY
SCHOLASTIC READER LVL 1: I SPY SANTA CLAUS

And for the Youngest Child:
I SPY LITTLE ANIMALS
I SPY LITTLE BOOK
I SPY LITTLE BUNNIES
I SPY LITTLE CHRISTMAS
I SPY LITTLE LEARNING BOX
I SPY LITTLE LETTERS
I SPY LITTLE NUMBERS
I SPY LITTLE WHEELS

Also Available:
I SPY CHALLENGER FOR GAME BOY ADVANCE
I SPY JUNIOR: PUPPET PLAYHOUSE CD-ROM
I SPY JUNIOR CD-ROM
I SPY SCHOOL DAYS CD-ROM
I SPY SPOOKY MANSION CD-ROM
I SPY TREASURE HUNT CD-ROM

I SPY
FANTASY

A BOOK OF PICTURE RIDDLES

Photographs by Walter Wick

Riddles by Jean Marzollo

Cartwheel ·B·O·O·K·S· ®

SCHOLASTIC INC.

New York   Toronto   London   Auckland   Sydney
Mexico City   New Delhi   Hong Kong   Buenos Aires

For Nancy Nina Chissotti (1936 – 1993)

W. W.

For Irene Trivas

J.M.

Book design by Carol Devine Carson

Text copyright © 1994 by Jean Marzollo.
Photographs copyright © 1994 by Walter Wick.
All rights reserved. Published by Scholastic Inc.

SCHOLASTIC, CARTWHEEL BOOKS, and associated logos
are trademarks and/or registered trademarks of Scholastic Inc.

Library of Congress Cataloging-in-Publication Data

Wick, Walter.
    I spy fantasy: a book of picture riddles / photographs by Walter
Wick; riddles by Jean Marzollo.
        p.   cm.
    ISBN 0-590-46295-4
    1. Picture puzzles — Juvenile literature. [1. Picture puzzles.]
    I. Marzollo, Jean.   II. Title.
GV1507.P47W522   1994
793.3–dc20   93-44814
                                                              CIP
                                                              AC

Reinforced Library Edition
ISBN-13: 978-0-439-68422-4
ISBN-10: 0-439-68422-6

10 9   13 14/0

Printed in Malaysia   108
This edition, March 2005

TABLE OF CONTENTS

Picture riddles fill this book;
Turn the pages! Take a look!

Use your mind, use your eye;
Read the riddles — play I SPY!

I spy a clock, a birdhouse, a duck,
Five thimbles, a plane, two fish in a truck;

A big red apple, a zebra jeep,
STOP, GO, and BEEP BEEP BEEP.

I spy a mailbox, a feather, a flute,
A horseshoe, a beetle, a basket of fruit;

Seven pinecones, an apron, a key,
A turtle, a swing, and the letter B.

I spy a fish, two rabbits, a kite,
A bear, a cat, and eight birds in flight;

A goose, a ship, a train, a sheep,
Eleven stars, and a baby asleep.

I spy eleven triangular blocks,
Twenty-six eyes, a whistle, two clocks;

An abacus face, two hot dogs, a hat,
BUMP, JUMP, YIKES! and a cat.

I spy two funnels, a flashlight, a cart,
An ice-cream scoop, a magnet, and START;

Six safety pins, a man on the run,
A plane, and the numbers from ten to one.

I spy a spider, a sea horse, a pear,
A horn, a frog, a pig, and a bear;

The sign for peace, a knight for chess,
Aladdin's lamp, and the letter S.

I spy a button, a rabbit, a snail,
A five, a straw, a little pink pail;

A bottle-cap knight, a key, and a bell,
A red lobster claw, and the poor knight who fell.

I spy a LAKE, five buttons, a four,
Three brushes, a comb, a musical score;

A spool of thread, a boot, an ace,
Six bobby pins, and a card from Grace.

I spy a fish, a rooster, a ring,
Five jelly beans, a star, and a king;

Three red crayons, shoelace hair,
A frightened tree, a bat, and BEWARE.

I spy a magnet, a fork, a kazoo,
A blue Scottie dog, a soccer ball, too;

A cat, a mouse, and part of a zipper,
A bunny, a swan, and the Little Dipper.

I spy a saucer, a gumball machine,
A camel, a melon, a race car that's green;

Eight small candles, a three-letter word,
A jelly-bean face, and a sweet yellow bird

I spy a turtle, a penny for a wish,
A door ajar, and a jewelry fish;

Four anchors, a ship, a shadowy whale,
A pot of gold, and A MERMAID'S TALE.

I spy a frog, and dinosaur bones,
Six hikers, a moose, a bat, two phones;

Three bears, a pencil, a monkey, a cart —
And in *each* picture, I spy a heart.

EXTRA CREDIT RIDDLES

 ## "Find Me" Riddle

I visit each picture and neigh, of course,

I'm Pegasus, the flying _____.

Find the Pictures That Go with These Riddles:

I spy a candle, a windmill, a spoon,

A boxing glove, and a crescent moon.

I spy an arrow, an underwater spring,

A fishhook, a phone, a shoe, and a ring.

I spy a turtle and a taxi cab,

A sandy star, and a curious crab.

I spy a flag, three stove knobs, a fork,

A caution sign, a cat, and a cork.

 I spy two mushrooms, an acorn, an owl,

A ball, three deer, and a little trowel.

I spy cake, a basket, a spoon,

A teapot, a pie, and a loose balloon.

I spy a paintbrush, a rolling shoe,

A fire hydrant, and two darts, too.

I spy a chair, an eight ball, a top,

A tree, a fish, a star, and STOP.

I spy a bugle, a zebra, a dime,

A parrot, a swan, and a note about time.

I spy a thumbtack, a four-leaf clover,

A man of stone, and a jar turned over.

I spy an airplane, a hot-air balloon,

A white butterfly, and the man in the moon.

I spy an owl, a snaky hose,

A blue paper clip, and six red toes.

I spy a fire truck, a blue hat, a shark,

An ice-cream cone, and a question mark.

Write Your Own Picture Riddles

There are many more hidden objects and many more possibilities for riddles in this book. Write some rhyming picture riddles yourself, and try them out with friends.

 # Write Your Own Stories

Use your imagination to make up stories and plays for the pictures in this book. There are no "right" answers — so be creative!

How *I Spy Fantasy* Was Made

 Walter Wick created the elaborate sets for *I Spy Fantasy* in his studio and then photographed them with an 8″ by 10″ view camera. Sets, such as *City Blocks, Blast Off!*, and *Into the Woods*, were formed with toys, household objects, and natural objects. To make the photograph for *Sand Castle*, Walter Wick had two tons of sand delivered to his studio. He dampened the sand and compressed it into a large wooden frame. The entire castle was carved from the compressed sand, with no glue added. The water and clouds in the background were painted on the sky-blue backdrop.

As the *I Spy Fantasy* sets were constructed, Walter Wick and Jean Marzollo conferred by phone and fax on the concepts for each picture and the objects to go in the sets, selecting the objects for their rhyming potential, as well as their aesthetic and playful qualities. Each finished set was lit by Walter Wick to create the right shadows, depth, and mood. For example, he

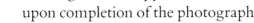

used dappled light to create the underwater effect in *The Deep Blue Sea*. Each set was dismantled before the next one was created. The sets survive only as photographs to inspire rhyming, riddle making, visual creativity, and the exciting challenge of the *I Spy* hunt. The final riddles were written upon completion of the photographs.

Walter Wick, the inventor of many photographic games for *Games* magazine, is the photographer of *I Spy: A Book of Picture Riddles*, *I Spy Christmas*, *I Spy Fun House*, and *I Spy Mystery*. He is also a free-lance photographer with credits including over 300 magazine and book covers, including *Newsweek*, *Discover*, *Psychology Today*, and Scholastic's *Let's Find Out* and *SuperScience*. This is his fifth book for Scholastic.

Jean Marzollo has written many rhyming children's books including the *I Spy* books, *In 1492*, *In 1776*, *Ten Cats Have Hats*, *Pretend You're a Cat*, and *Close Your Eyes*. She is also the author of *My First Book of Biographies* and *Happy Birthday, Martin Luther King*. **Carol Devine Carson**, the book designer for the *I Spy* series, is art director for a major publishing house in New York City. For nineteen years, Marzollo and Carson produced Scholastic's kindergarten magazine, *Let's Find Out*.

Acknowledgments

We are deeply grateful for the support and assistance of Grace Maccarone, Bernette Ford, Edie Weinberg, and many others at Scholastic; Molly Friedrich at Aaron M. Priest Agency, Linda Cheverton-Wick, Kevin Williams, Bob Pirla, Maria McGowan, Frank and Ray Hills, and the Nutmeg Ballet Company in Torrington, CT. We'd also like to extend a special thanks to artist Bruce Morozko, who helped with the sets for *Sand Castle, Blast Off!*, and *The Rainbow Express*.

Walter Wick and Jean Marzollo